Gypsy Rose and the Mother's Odyssey

A Saga of Betrayal, Liberation, and Unraveled Secrets

Copyright

Copyright © 2023, by John Gragg. All rights reserved. No part of this book may be reproduced, stored in a retrieval system, or transmitted in any form or by any means, electronic, mechanical, photocopying, recording, scanning, or otherwise, except as permitted under Section 107 or 108 of the 1976 United States Copyright Act, without the prior written permission of the author

Table of Contents

Introduction

Chapter One
> Dee Dee's initial claims about Gypsy's health
>> Gypsy's early years subjected to unnecessary medical interventions, fabrications of Gypsy's illnesses and manipulation of medical professionals and caregivers by her mother (Dee Dee)

Chapter Two
> Life in the Facade and the Breaking Point
>> Gypsy's life under the constant deception, medical treatments, Signs of resistance and attempts to escape.

Chapter Three
> Online Escapade and The Murder Plot with Nicholas Godejohm

Gypsy's online encounters and the formation of a plan, Introduction of Nicholas Godejohn and the events leading to Dee Dee's murder

Chapter Four
Legal Proceeding and Life in Jail

Chapter Five
Aftermath and Revelations
Truth revealed and Gypsy's realization of the extent of her mother's deception

Chapter Six
Life After Prison
Gypsy's life now including statements on her post-prison life and newfound freedom

Chapter Seven
FAQ regarding the case and people's reactions including on X Platform

Conclusion

Request

Introduction

In the heart of Springfield, Missouri, a captivating story unfolds, a story about Gypsy Rose and her mother, a tale that pulls back the curtain on a life filled with secrets and illusions, a tale that would grip the world with its twists and turns, exposing the fragility of trust and the shadows cast by a mother's deception.

Picture a young woman named Gypsy Rose, navigating a life where every breath was drawn within the confines of her mother's intricate web of lies. The world saw a wheelchair-bound, frail figure battling a myriad of illnesses, but beneath the surface, a different narrative was silently unfolding.

Gypsy Rose Blanchard grew up with her mom, Dee Dee Blanchard, always saying she was sick, leading to lots of serious diagnoses and treatments. But here's the twist; Gypsy wasn't actually sick. Her mom had been making up for all those symptoms.

Experts think Dee Dee's actions were driven by a mental disorder called Munchausen syndrome by proxy. Basically, Dee Dee pretended Gypsy was sick because she wanted to take care of her.

The shocking truth about Gypsy and her mom only came out when Gypsy arranged for her online boyfriend to do something drastic and harm her mom in 2015. This sad story unfolds the complicated relationship between a mother and daughter, filled with lies, deceit, and an unexpected turn of events.

The epic saga of Gypsy Rose Blanchard and her mother, shrouded in a veneer of devoted care and relentless medical interventions, reveals a story that transcends the boundaries of a conventional narrative. It's a tale of a daughter ensnared in the clutches of her mother's illusions, a story that unravels layer by layer, exposing the depths of deception.

As we embark on this journey, we delve into the moments that defined Gypsy's existence; the whispered secrets, the fabricated ailments, and the silent plea for liberation. This is not just a story of betrayal; it's an exploration of the human spirit, resilience in the face of adversity, and the complexities that bind a mother and daughter.

Join me as we unravel the enigma of Gypsy Rose and the Mother's Odyssey; an odyssey that spans deception, liberation, and the untangling of secrets that echo through the corridors of time.

Chapter One

Dee Dee's initial claims about Gypsy's health

Gypsy's early years subjected to unnecessary medical interventions, fabrications of Gypsy's illnesses and manipulation of medical professionals and caregivers by her mother (Dee Dee)

Gypsy Rose Blanchard grew up with her mom, Dee Dee Blanchard, always saying she was sick, leading to lots of serious diagnoses and treatments. But here's the twist; Gypsy wasn't actually sick. Her mom had been making up for all those symptoms.

Experts think Dee Dee's actions were driven by a mental disorder called Munchausen syndrome by proxy.

Basically, Dee Dee pretended Gypsy was sick because she wanted to take care of her.

The shocking truth about Gypsy and her mom only came out when Gypsy arranged for her online boyfriend to do something drastic and harm her mom in 2015. This sad story unfolds the complicated relationship between a mother and daughter, filled with lies, deceit, and an unexpected turn of events.

Dee Dee's intricate web of deception took root from the very early days of Gypsy Rose's life. Born in 1991, Gypsy was just a baby when her mother began fabricating a series of illnesses. Dee Dee's imaginative narrative commenced with the claim that Gypsy suffered from sleep apnea, a condition diagnosed in infancy.

However, as Gypsy grew, the list of concocted ailments expanded exponentially.

By the time Gypsy reached the tender age of 8, Dee Dee had painted a vivid picture of a child grappling with leukemia and muscular dystrophy. According to her mother's intricate storyline, Gypsy needed a wheelchair and a feeding tube to navigate daily life. The list of fabricated medical problems did not end there; it extended to encompass seizures, asthma, as well as hearing and visual impairments.

Dee Dee's elaborate charade not only subjected Gypsy to a plethora of false diagnoses but also led to a cascade of medical interventions. Gypsy found herself entangled in a complex world of prescriptions, compelled to use a breathing machine for sleep.

The extent of Dee Dee's deception even reached invasive surgical procedures, including operations on Gypsy's eyes and the removal of her salivary glands. The toll of this elaborate ruse manifested in the decay of Gypsy's teeth, prompting the painful necessity of extraction—perhaps a consequence of medications, absent salivary glands, or an unfortunate result of neglect.

The stark reality contrasted sharply with the elaborate fiction spun by Dee Dee. Despite the intricately woven narrative of Gypsy's severe health issues, the truth unveiled a starkly different picture. Gypsy, in fact, possessed the ability to walk, had no need for a feeding tube, and was not battling cancer. The apparent hair loss was not a result of any medical condition; rather, it was a consequence of her mother shaving off her hair.

The experts postulate that Dee Dee's actions were driven by a mental illness known as Munchausen syndrome by proxy, a condition where a caregiver fabricates or induces illness in someone under their care, often to garner attention and sympathy.

Dee Dee's facade as a charming and devoted mother cast a veil over the deception. Medical examinations frequently produced inconclusive or contradictory results regarding Gypsy's supposed ailments, yet Dee Dee strategically avoided any doctors who dared to question her narrative.

Complicit caregivers, influenced by Dee Dee's purported expertise gained from some nurse's training, willingly adhered to her wishes. Dee Dee's charm extended to her interactions with medical professionals, where she aptly described symptoms and, shockingly, even administered medication to Gypsy to mimic specific conditions.

Guiding the narrative with a facade of maternal dedication, Dee Dee ensured that Gypsy adhered to a scripted version of her own medical history. Instructing her daughter not to volunteer information during medical appointments, Dee Dee skillfully crafted a narrative that perpetuated the illusion of Gypsy's numerous fabricated ailments. This chapter in Gypsy's life unravels the layers of manipulation, showcasing Dee Dee's ability to weave a captivating story that ensnared not only her daughter but also those in her trusted circle.

Gypsy Rose Blanchard

Chapter Two

Life in the Facade and the Breaking Point

Gypsy's life under the constant deception, medical treatments, Signs of resistance and attempts to escape.

Dee Dee's web of deceit extended beyond her immediate household, ensnaring even Gypsy's father, Rod Blanchard. Dee Dee informed Rod that their daughter was afflicted with a chromosomal disorder, attributing it to the root cause of her numerous health issues. Rather than questioning the validity of these claims, Rod praised Dee Dee for her seemingly devoted care.

However, as suspicions began to arise within Dee Dee's own family, prompted by the observation that Gypsy did not appear to require a wheelchair, Dee Dee swiftly devised a solution—she and Gypsy uprooted their lives and relocated.

Under the guise of escaping scrutiny, Dee Dee concocted yet another narrative, claiming to be a victim of Hurricane Katrina. This tragic event provided the perfect cover for Dee Dee and Gypsy to receive assistance in relocating from Louisiana to Missouri in 2005.

Unfazed by the change in location, Dee Dee seamlessly continued her practice of bringing Gypsy to numerous doctor's appointments. The aftermath of Hurricane Katrina conveniently served as an excuse for missing medical files, shielding Dee Dee's elaborate deception from closer scrutiny.

As Gypsy transitioned into adolescence, Dee Dee's fabricated narrative persisted, with claims of ongoing illnesses and a deliberate distortion of Gypsy's age. In 2008, mother and daughter relocated to a new home in Springfield, Missouri—a dwelling constructed by Habitat for Humanity, adorned in pink, and equipped with a wheelchair ramp.

This change of scenery did not deter Dee Dee's pursuit of benefits, including sponsored visits to concerts and Disney World, all while she continued to revel in the attention showered upon her as a purportedly devoted caretaker.

At the age of 14, Gypsy sought the expertise of a neurologist in Missouri, who, upon careful examination, suspected that Gypsy was a victim of Munchausen syndrome by proxy. However, despite harboring these concerns, the neurologist refrained from reporting the case to authorities, citing insufficient evidence to support such action. In 2009, an anonymous report surfaced, challenging the validity of Dee Dee's accounts regarding Gypsy's medical conditions. Two caseworkers were dispatched to investigate, yet Dee Dee skillfully persuaded them that all was well, deflecting any potential interference in her carefully constructed facade.

As Gypsy matured, Dee Dee's tactics evolved, encompassing further deceit about her daughter's age. Resorting to altering Gypsy's birth certificate to create the illusion of a younger child, Dee Dee found herself facing an escalating challenge—Gypsy was gradually slipping beyond her control.

This period in Gypsy's life exposes the increasing complexity of the web Dee Dee had woven and the mounting difficulty she encountered in managing the evolving narrative surrounding her daughter.

Gypsy Rose Blanchard

Chapter Three

Online Escapade and The Murder Plot with Nicholas Godejohm

Gypsy's online encounters and the formation of a plan, Introduction of Nicholas Godejohn and the events leading to Dee Dee's murder

In a desperate bid for freedom in 2011, Gypsy attempted to escape her mother's clutches by eloping with a man she had met at a science fiction convention. Their escape, however, was short-lived, as Dee Dee swiftly located them through mutual acquaintances. Manipulating the situation, Dee Dee convinced the man that Gypsy was a minor, despite the reality that she was 19 at the time. Upon their return home, Gypsy faced a harrowing ordeal—Dee Dee allegedly smashed her computer and physically restrained her to the bed. Gypsy recounted instances of her mother's physical abuse, including being denied food.

Later on Gypsy met Nicholas Godejohn online whom she divulged the painful truth about her mother's actions. As their connection deepened, Gypsy made a shocking request—she asked Godejohn to eliminate Dee Dee from their lives so they could be together.

In June 2015, Godejohn carried out this chilling request, entering Gypsy's house and fatally stabbing Dee Dee, while Gypsy, ears covered, awaited the resolution in the bathroom. This pivotal moment in Gypsy's life marks a disturbing turning point, revealing the extreme measures she felt compelled to take in order to liberate herself from the confines of her mother's manipulation.

Gypsy Rose Blanchard detailed the genesis of her relationship with Nicholas Godejohn, recounting that they first connected on a Christian dating website in 2012. Their clandestine romance unfolded through text messages, which were later scrutinized during Godejohn's trial. Prosecutors argued that Godejohn meticulously plotted for over a year before carrying out the stabbing of Clauddine Blanchard. His defense countered, asserting that Godejohn's autism impeded the mental capabilities required for premeditation.

Their first in-person encounter occurred in March 2015 when Godejohn traveled from Wisconsin to meet Gypsy. Text messages presented during the trial unveiled the evolving dynamics of their relationship, encompassing discussions about love, intimacy, and plans for a shared future.

However, a stark shift occurred in June 2015, as their conversations turned darker, with mentions of the necessity for duct tape and knives in the days leading up to Clauddine (Dee Dee) Blanchard's demise. Godejohn and Gypsy referred to each other's darker impulses—Godejohn's "evil side" that he claimed "enjoys killing," and Gypsy's darker persona named "Ruby."

Clauddine Blanchard's lifeless body was discovered after her friends noticed a concerning post on her Facebook page, declaring, "That (expletive) is dead." When Gypsy testified at Godejohn's trial, she admitted to influencing him, asserting, "I talked him into it." Godejohn's defense posited that his profound love and obsession for Gypsy, coupled with his autism, rendered him susceptible to manipulation.

Prosecutors, however, contended that his motivations were rooted in sexual desire and the quest to be with Gypsy. The probable cause statement indicated that Gypsy provided the knife and concealed herself in a bathroom while Godejohn repeatedly stabbed her mother.

Subsequently, the two fled to Wisconsin by bus, where they were eventually apprehended. Gypsy later clarified that her provocative online posts were strategically crafted to ensure the discovery of her mother's body. This intricate web of emotions, manipulation, and sinister planning underscores the complex narrative surrounding Gypsy and Godejohn's actions.

Chapter Four

Legal Proceeding and Life in Jail

In a twist of fate, Gypsy Rose Blanchard found a glimmer of justice as prosecutors acknowledged the years of abuse she had endured. In 2016, she struck a deal, pleading guilty to second-degree murder, a compromise that spared her a life sentence. The initial looming threat of a first-degree murder charge, which could have resulted in a lifetime behind bars, was averted. Gypsy's then-boyfriend, Nicholas Godejohn, wasn't as fortunate, receiving a life sentence for his involvement in the chilling act.

The transformation Gypsy underwent in prison is both physical and symbolic.

Liberated from the constraints of her mother's control, she emerged with her hair grown and the ability to walk unaided by a wheelchair. Her attorney, Mike Stanfield, highlighted the rarity of a client looking "exceedingly better" after an extended prison term, emphasizing the toll her past life had taken on her well-being. The visible change serves as a testament to the severity of the challenges Gypsy faced and ultimately overcame.

Despite the adversity, Gypsy Rose Blanchard found an unexpected chapter of her life unfolding even within prison walls. While incarcerated, she forged a connection that defied the shadows of her haunting past. Gypsy married Ryan Scott Anderson, a poignant symbol of newfound love and a glimmer of hope amid the echoes of a troubled history. The union, albeit in the confines of prison, represents a paradoxical juxtaposition of liberation and constraint, mirroring Gypsy's complex journey from captivity to a semblance of freedom.

Gypsy Rose Blanchard

Chapter Five

Aftermath and Revelations

Truth revealed and Gypsy's realization of the extent of her mother's deception

In the aftermath of Dee Dee's murder, Gypsy Rose Blanchard found herself grappling with an overwhelming sense of fear and isolation. Despite the perplexity of why she resorted to such a drastic act, Gypsy's explanation unveiled the deep-seated psychological chains that bound her. The fear of exposing her mother's lies was paralyzing; Gypsy believed she had no one to trust, leaving her entangled in a web of apprehension.

The post-murder scrutiny from those who knew her raised questions about why Gypsy hadn't simply stood up against the deception. However, Gypsy's poignant revelation painted a picture of a life marred by conditioned fear and a profound lack of trust.

Gypsy's life had been a narrative of control and monitoring orchestrated by Dee Dee. Denied the opportunity to attend school, Gypsy's intelligence was overshadowed by her mother's fabricated narrative, proclaiming her to have a mental age of 7. The public facade involved constant hand-holding, a stifling gesture signaling Gypsy to be silent.

Dr. Marc Feldman, an authority on Munchausen syndrome by proxy, drew a chilling parallel, describing Gypsy as essentially a hostage. The metaphor of a kidnapped victim reflected the totality of control that Dee Dee wielded over her daughter, offering a grim lens through which to understand the desperate act of liberation Gypsy sought.

Gypsy Rose Blanchard

Chapter Six

Life After Prison

Gypsy's life now including statements on her post-prison life and newfound freedom

Gypsy Rose Blanchard's release from prison on December 28, 2023, marked a pivotal moment in her life after serving eight years for her role in her mother's tragic murder. The Missouri Department of Corrections confirmed her release from Chillicothe Correctional Center around 3:30 a.m. local time. As Gypsy stepped out into newfound freedom, she was met by her husband, Ryan Scott Anderson, a supportive figure who had been a steadfast emotional anchor throughout her incarceration.

Ryan, a 37-year-old middle school special education teacher from Louisiana, played a crucial role in Gypsy's journey towards recovery and rehabilitation. Their connection began with a letter sent by Ryan in 2020, and over the years, he evolved into an essential source of strength for Gypsy. As they embarked on the next chapter of their lives together, Gypsy expressed deep gratitude for Ryan, acknowledging his unwavering support during the challenging years leading up to her release.

In 2016, facing the charges related to Dee Dee's death, Gypsy entered into a plea deal arranged by her lawyer. Pleading guilty to second-degree murder, she received a 10-year prison sentence, of which she served 85 percent before her release on December 28, 2023. Meanwhile, Godejohn, her accomplice, was found guilty of first-degree murder in 2018 and received a life sentence.

After Dee Dee's demise, Gypsy's perspective on her mother's elaborate deceit became clearer. Realizing the extent of the falsehoods surrounding her health, Gypsy, who had been aware of her ability to walk and consume regular food, had been under the impression she had leukemia.

As she stepped into her newfound freedom, Gypsy reflected on her time in prison, expressing that she found a degree of liberation behind bars compared to the constrained life she shared with Dee Dee. However, when questioned about her feelings toward her mother's death, Gypsy conveyed a complex sentiment: "I'm glad that I'm out of that situation, but I'm not happy she's dead." Eagerly anticipating a reunion, Gypsy expressed her desire to reconnect with her father, stepmother, and her husband.

Gypsy Rose Blanchard is already diving into new endeavors as she embraces her freedom. Her e-book, "Released: Conversations on the Eve of Freedom," is slated for publication by Penguin Random House on January 9, 2024. Co-authored, the biography features exclusive in-prison interviews, insights into her personal life, and a visual journey through Gypsy's experiences, including photos and sketches.

Additionally, a Lifetime docu-series titled "The Prison Confessions of Gypsy

Rose Blanchard" is scheduled to premiere on January 5, 2024, providing an in-depth exploration of Gypsy's life.

Beyond literary and screen projects, Gypsy reveals a personal connection to Taylor Swift's music. She used the money her father sent her in prison to purchase Taylor Swift's albums, finding solace in the artist's songs. Gypsy has plans to attend a Chiefs game, aiming to meet Taylor Swift, emphasizing the impact Swift's song "Eyes Open" had on helping her overcome trauma from her mother's abuse.

Gypsy Rose Blanchard

Chapter Seven

FAQ regarding the case and people's reactions including on X Platform

The FAQ
- What medical procedures were performed on Gypsy Rose?

Gypsy Blanchard underwent unnecessary medical procedures, including the removal of her salivary glands. Her mother manipulated doctors into believing these procedures were necessary, using a topical anesthetic to induce drooling. Essentially, Gypsy's mother kept her in a state of captivity.

- How old is Gypsy Rose in 2023?

As of 2023, Gypsy Blanchard is 32 years old. She was born on July 27, 1991.

- What kind of abuse did Gypsy Rose face from her mother?

As Gypsy Rose grew older, she testified that the abuse from her mother escalated to physical violence. She recounted instances where her mother beat her and even chained her to a bed.

- Who is Gypsy Rose married to?

She is married to Ryan, a 37-year-old middle school special education teacher from Louisiana. Gypsy Rose expressed her anticipation of returning to a supportive family dynamic with her husband. She emphasized the importance of having this supportive structure that she felt was missing throughout her ordeal.

- Why did Gypsy Rose undergo the removal of all her teeth?

Dee Dee opted to have all of Gypsy's teeth extracted after dentists discovered one tooth decaying in her mouth.

- How old was Dee Dee when she passed away?

Dee Dee Blanchard was 48 years old when she died in 2015 (1967–2015).

- How were Gypsy and Godejohn caught?

After tracking the through Facebook posts made by Gypsy, the police raided Godejohn's home on June 15, 2015. Godejohn surrendered and was taken into custody, while Gypsy was found unharmed and subsequently arrested.

- How did Gypsy discover her real age?

As of March 2019, the authentic Gypsy Rose is 27 years old, now 32. She learned about her true age at 19 when she found her real birth certificate from 1991, causing her to question her mother. Dee Dee dismissed it as a typo.

- At what age did Gypsy commit the crime?

When Dee Dee Blanchard was found dead in June 2015, Gypsy, aged 23 at the time, and her then-boyfriend, Nick Godejohn, were both charged with murder.

- Why did Dee Dee mistreat Gypsy?

Experts believe Dee Dee suffered from Munchausen syndrome by proxy, a mental illness where she fabricated her daughter's illnesses to garner attention and sympathy for being a caretaker of a supposedly sick child.

Public Reaction on X Platform

"Overwhelmingly happy for her. I hope she gets to live the next chapter of her life exactly how she wants."

"She's a queen for admitting that and speaking her truth. I hope she has a happy life starting tomorrow."

"Life rarely gives us second chances. I hope Gypsy Rose can return to society and make the best of this second chance."

"She's right but it's still understandable why she did what she did at the time. I hope she has forgiven herself."

"You're not capable of making proper judgments when you've been abused for so long. Poor thing. She was like a caged animal backed up against a wall and she didn't know how to defend herself + the system was broken and enabled her abuser. I hope she forgives herself."

"I think she has! Understanding you'd done something wrong doesn't always indicate guilt. I think it's very healthy to acknowledge she was in a horrible situation and did a horrible thing to get out of it. I'm just wishing her well moving forward!"

"She has clearly grown and sounds well rehabilitated. I wish her a good life starting tomorrow."

"Gypsy Rose Blanchard's statement reflects a complex and tragic situation. It's a reminder of the intricate dynamics involved in cases like hers, where the lines between victim and perpetrator are blurred."

"Having to kill your parents is one of the greatest burdens one can carry. You cannot run away from it or even choose to dissociate from it because it involves someone who you thought was meant to take care of you and love you."

"I'm proud of her & her mother DID DESERVE THAT. Any human being that can physically hurt a child in any way deserves that. I really hope she stays off social media tho".

"She did what she had to do but I can appreciate her honesty and openness. FREE HER UNTIL IT'S BACKWARDS"

Conclusion

In the aftermath of the tumultuous events that unfolded in the life of Gypsy Rose Blanchard, the complexity of human nature and the enduring impact of manipulation come sharply into focus. Gypsy's journey from a life shrouded in deception and control to the stark reality of a prison cell, and eventually, her emergence into a world without the oppressive grasp of her mother, forms a poignant narrative.

As we reflect on the layers of this true-life story, one is compelled to consider the blurred lines between victim and perpetrator. Gypsy's actions, driven by a desperate need for liberation, unveil the depths of her captivity. Dr. Marc Feldman's analogy, likening her situation to that of a hostage, resonates profoundly. Gypsy's world, dictated by the whims of her mother's fabrications, was a prison of its own making.

The psychological intricacies of Munchausen syndrome by proxy, as expertly articulated by Dr. Feldman and others, underscore the tragedy that unfolded. Dee Dee's relentless pursuit of sympathy and attention cast a shadow over Gypsy's entire existence, leaving her ensnared in a web of lies.

As Gypsy navigates her newfound freedom, the conflicting emotions surrounding her mother's demise echo the tumult within. The revelation of the extent of Dee Dee's deception after her death casts a haunting light on the years of manipulation and control.

In the legal arena, Gypsy's plea deal and Nicholas Godejohn's trial lay bare the complexities of justice. The courtroom becomes a stage where the shades of morality and motive intertwine, leaving us to grapple with the implications of their actions.

Yet, as the narrative concludes, the story of Gypsy Rose Blanchard is not merely a tale of tragedy but a testament to resilience. Gypsy, now free from the shackles of her past, stands as a symbol of courage in the face of insurmountable odds. The intricacies of her psyche, the scars of her past, and the complexity of her emotions paint a portrait of a survivor emerging from the shadows.

In this final chapter, we bear witness to the lingering questions that resonate with the reader. What lessons can be gleaned from the tragedy that unfolded within the Blanchard household? How can society better recognize and intervene in cases of profound manipulation and abuse?

The Gypsy Rose Blanchard story invites contemplation on the fragility of trust, the intricacies of the human mind, and the resilience of the human spirit. As the curtain falls on this gripping narrative, it leaves us not only with a sense of closure but also with a profound appreciation for the indomitable strength that can arise from the darkest depths of deception.

Request

Dear Valued Reader,

Your feedback and support mean the world to me as an author committed to providing valuable books to readers like you.

If you've found this book helpful, I kindly ask you to consider sharing your thoughts in the form of a review on Amazon. Your 5-star ratings and positive reviews go a long way in helping others discover and benefit from the book's content.

Your feedback not only supports my work as an author but also serves as a valuable resource for prospective readers. Whether you found the book insightful, informative, or simply enjoyed the journey it took you on, your words can make a difference.

Thank you for being a part of this incredible community of readers. Your engagement and support are deeply appreciated. I look forward to hearing your thoughts and hope you continue to find inspiration and joy throughout your life.

Warm regards,
John Gragg
Thank you.

Printed in Great Britain
by Amazon